GOAL!
LATIN STARS OF
SOCCER

Soccer Star

Robinho

Marty Gitlin

Robinho Star
Keep Boys Reading!

Speeding Star, an imprint of Enslow Publishers, Inc.

Library of Congress Cataloging-in-Publication Data

Gitlin, Marty.
Soccer star Robinho / Marty Gitlin.
pages cm. — (Goal! Latin stars of soccer)
Includes bibliographical references and index.
Summary: "Brazilian soccer star Robinho was born into a family with little money and not many options for a good life. In this sports biography, explore how with the help of soccer legend Pelé, Robinho has been able to not only become wealthy but become one of the best soccer players in the world"—Provided by publisher.
ISBN 978-1-62285-216-1
1. Souza, Robson de, 1984—Juvenile literature. 2. Soccer players—Brazil—Biography. I. Title.
GV942.7.R57G58 2013
796.334092—dc23
[B]
                                2013018205

Future Editions:
Paperback ISBN: 978-1-62285-217-8
EPUB ISBN: 978-1-62285-218-5
Single-User PDF ISBN: 978-1-62285-219-2
Multi-User PDF ISBN: 978-1-62285-220-8

Printed in the United States of America
112013 Bang Printing, Brainerd, Minn.
10 9 8 7 6 5 4 3 2 1

Speeding Star
Box 398, 40 Industrial Road
Berkeley Heights, NJ 07922
USA
www.speedingstar.com

Photo Credits: ©AP Images/Alexandre Meneghini, p. 20; ©AP Images/Andre Penner, p. 40; ©AP Images/Antonio Calanni, p. 7; ©AP Images/Bernat Armangue, pp. 25, 28; ©AP Images/Claudio Cruz, p. 4; ©AP Images/Dado Galdieri, p. 23; ©AP Images/Fernando Llano, p. 13; ©AP Images/Juan Manuel Serrano, p. 31; ©AP Images/Jorge Saenz, p. 17; ©AP Images/Luca Bruno, p. 43; ©AP Images/Manu Fernandez, p. 27; ©AP Images/Marcelo Hernandez, p. 14; ©AP Images/Maurico de Souza/Agencia Estado, p. 19; ©AP Images/Natacha Pisarenko, p. 11; ©AP Images/Nelson Antoine, p. 8; ©AP Images/Paul Thomas, p. 35; ©AP Images/Philippos Christou, p. 33; ©AP Images/Stephan Savoia, p. 44; ©AP Images/Wander Roberto/Agencia Estado, p. 36.

Cover Photo: ©AP Images/Martin Meissner

CONTENTS

Robinho kicks his second goal against Chile in the Copa América tournament and would go on to finish with three goals on the day.

Giving Brazil a Thrill

It was July 1, 2007. More than fifty thousand screaming fans packed the soccer stadium in Venezuela. The national teams from Brazil and Chile were battling in the Copa América, or America Cup.

Six minutes remained in the game. The outcome was still in doubt. Brazil held a 1–0 lead. Striker Robinho had scored the only goal.

He knew the lead was not safe so he did something about it. He bolted past a defender and found an open space in front of the net. He received a pass as Chile's goaltender, Claudio Bravo, raced forward to try to block his shot. Bravo was too late. Robinho blasted the ball past and over him for another goal. Brazil 2, Chile 0.

Robinho was just warming up. It was time to clinch the victory. A minute later, he tricked one defender by sliding the ball past him. He used his amazing skill to secure it from another Chilean player. He centered it in front of the net and booted it past the diving Bravo.

Soon the game was over. Robinho had scored every goal in a 3–0 win. And he stayed red-hot. He played hero for Brazil again three days later against Ecuador.

That game was scoreless early in the second half. Robinho sprang into action. He prepared for a penalty kick that could give his team the lead. He stared at Ecuador goalkeeper Marcelo Elizaga. He rushed forward and blasted the ball. Elizaga dove to his left. But Robinho had placed his kick perfectly. The ball zoomed into the corner of the net. The Brazilian fans screamed with delight. They roared even louder as their team completed the 1–0 victory.

If the Chilean players thought Robinho was done tormenting them, they were wrong. They had the bad luck of playing Brazil in the next round of the Copa América. The twenty-three-year-old superstar was again on top of his game. He displayed his quickness by faking out a defender and booting the ball into the net for a goal.

He was overcome with joy, so he broke into a dance of celebration. He was showing the sense of fun he had always had playing this sport. He later scored again in an easy 6–1 win.

Robinho was the star of the event. He had scored six goals in just four games, including all four that Brazil tallied in the first round. He was trying to break the tournament record of eight. The mark, set in 1959 by Brazil's legendary Pelé, was important. Soccer fans in that country saw Robinho as their next great superstar. He was going to be the new Pelé.

The twenty-three-year-old did not tie or break the record. But he did help Brazil win its fourth title in the last five Copa Américas.

Most believed his team would lose to Argentina in the championship match. After all, top players Ronaldinho and Kaká were injured and out of action. Argentina had won all five of its matches by a combined score of 16–3. But when the ball had stopped bouncing, Brazil had a 3–0

The excitement that Robinho displays after he scores shows that he truly loves playing soccer and has fun while doing it.

victory. The team had the eighth America Cup crown in its rich soccer history.

It would not have been possible without Robinho. He had provided badly needed offense when none of his teammates were scoring. The exciting striker had dominated the first two rounds. He had won the Golden Boot Award as the top scorer of the event. And it was no surprise when he was honored as its best player.

Robinho led the 2007 Copa América in goals scored. But he had also proven himself as much more than a scorer. Some who watched his wizardry with the ball believed he was the most talented dribbler in the sport. He showed off his skills as a passer. He displayed his all-around play. His performance opened the eyes of fans, teammates, and opponents. Some believed that Robinho was now the best player in the world.

Soccer legend Pelé is one of the biggest reasons that Robinho has become a star in the soccer world.

But when it was over, he did not speak about himself. He talked instead about what his team had achieved. He was proud that Brazil had overcome poor play to win the title.

"This was a group that worked and fought loads and knew that we had to get better," he said. "We achieved our objective. He had problems since the beginning. We knew it was going to be difficult but we achieved our objective."

Robinho had been working to achieve his objectives for a long time. He had been dubbed the next Pelé many years before leading Brazil to the 2007 Copa América title.

Poor Child, Rich Talent

There was a reason Robinho spent his childhood kicking soccer balls or flying a paper kite. Those activities cost little money. His parents had little money. They could not afford to buy their child a bicycle or other fun toys.

Robinho was born Robson de Souza on January 25, 1984. He was raised in the poor Parque Bitaru section of São Vicente, Brazil. He was a tiny child living in a tiny home. His father, Gilvan, who toiled as a sewer worker, slept in the same room as wife Marina and their son.

They were not alone in their money misery. Nearly half of all Brazilians are very poor. About 40 percent earn less than 46 dollars a month. For millions of children from that country, soccer is the only legal escape. Many others turn to crime.

The boy, nicknamed Robinho because of his slight build, was not one of them. He spent most of his time

Robinho is shown holding his trophy, the Golden Boot, for being the top scorer in the 2007 Copa América.

dribbling a soccer ball on the street. He ate very little. His diet consisted mostly of rice and eggs. But his dedication soon paid off. He had developed a special talent by the age of six. His skills were already far better than those of his friends. But some believed his size would prevent him from beating bigger, stronger players.

"When I was younger they used to tell me that I'm too thin and it would be hard for me to compete," Robinho said. "But I've never had any difficulty playing, playing offense, dribbling. I think [soccer] players are becoming bigger overall. But I think strength will never beat intelligence. If you're smart, the defense will not stop you!"

He was convinced at age six to join Beira-Mar. The soccer club trains teams for local junior leagues. Robinho did not play at the same level with others his age. He helped his team win a championship in his first season.

Robinho gained agility and dribbling skills through futsal—a form of soccer played on a basketball court. It is a much faster sport than soccer which is played on large fields. It requires speed and quickness. Robinho showed more talent as a dribbler than his teammates and opponents. Beira-Mar coordinator, Adroaldo Ricardo, recalled the first time he watched Robinho perform.

"The first time he got the ball we realized that he was different from the others," Ricardo said. "He would make these spectacular moves."

His parents were against him joining Beira-Mar. But they soon noticed their son's skills and the attention he

What separates Robinho from other superstars is that he takes time everywhere he goes to sign autographs for his fans.

received. They saw in him an escape from poverty. He was so talented that Beira-Mar stopped charging his family its monthly fee. His parents could not afford his bus fare to the club, so a neighbor stepped in to pay it.

Robinho was too young to understand, though. He was not driven by saving his family. He played for his love of the game. He enjoyed creating new moves with a soccer ball. He dreamed of becoming a star.

Ricardo was not alone among those who noticed his gift for soccer. Coach Betinho Rocha was impressed with his talent. He was also amazed by how much confidence Robinho had at a young age.

After winning the 2007 Copa América, Robinho and his teammates celebrate their victory with the trophy.

"Robinho was different from the others," Rocha said. "He had no fear of his opponents."

Robinho rose quickly through the ranks of youth soccer. He was moved to a higher-level futsal club called Portuários at age nine. Professional scouts started taking notice when he scored an incredible 73 goals in one season.

The media coverage also brought attention. A reporter interviewed Robinho after one game in which he scored two goals to lead his team to victory. Soon he was invited to play on the futsal club in the bigger city of Santos.

That is when fate stepped in. Pelé ran the youth program in that town. The Brazilian soccer legend took Robinho under his wing. Pelé praised the boy by comparing him to himself as a young player. Pelé even formed a friendship with Robinho's father. He told Gilvan that he was going to give Robinho special attention.

Robinho was excited. He was flattered that perhaps the greatest soccer player in history would pick him out among all the young soccer players in the Santos program. He was happy just to have met Pelé. He would never forget their first meeting.

"I never thought I'd meet the King of [Soccer] at that stage," Robinho said. "He praised me and gave me some advice. He said that if I had the humility and calmness I stood a very good chance of becoming a pro."

Robinho was about to become more than just a professional soccer player. He was on the verge of growing into a superstar.

New Life for Robinho

The days of bouncing a soccer ball as he walked along the cobbled streets of Parque Bitaru were over for Robinho in 1999.

He moved that year into a home for promising teenage players run by the Santos Futebol Clube. He was eating three square meals a day for the first time in his life. He slept in a small dorm room. He and his fellow young prospects were kept busy at all times so they would stay out of trouble.

Greedy agents often present problems for poor, young players. They lure away kids as young as fourteen years old to Europe. It is usually proven there that they are not ready

Futsal was a huge help in training Robinho to become one of the quickest and most agile dribblers in international soccer.

to compete. Their agents then abandon them. The boys are left in Europe, thousands of miles away from home without money. Three of the players Robinho competed with at Beira-Mar wound up playing in Guatemala, a poorer country than Brazil.

Pelé would not allow that to happen to Robinho. The soccer legend conditioned the skinny boy with the amazing moves. Robinho made enough progress to debut with the Santos top team at age eighteen. He teamed with fellow young star Diego da Cunha to lead Santos to the 2002 Campeonato Brasileiro Série A, or simply, the Brazilian national title.

Fans were in awe of Robinho's ability to juke defenders. He tricked opponents with fancy dribbling that had been a trademark of the finest players in Brazil for many years. In the title game against heated rival Corinthians, he eluded star fullback Rogério eight times. Rogério grew frustrated and committed a penalty. Robinho scored on the penalty kick. That goal gave Santos the momentum to run away with the victory.

The media dubbed Robinho the "Stepover King" for the move that fooled Rogério time and again. They also called him a soccer genius, just as they had Pelé fifty years earlier. The championship won by Santos was its first in eighteen years. Robinho was voted the best striker in Brazil after that season. That meant he won the Bola de Prata, or Silver ball for being the best striker in the Brazil National Championship.

This photo of Robinho and his mother became an iconic image during her kidnapping that shook the entire soccer world.

He was among the top scorers on the Santos team in 2002 and 2003. But it was not just his ability to put the ball in the net that fans loved. They were entertained by his style on the soccer field. Even the opposing fans showed their appreciation for his amazing skills. He received a standing ovation during a 2002 game against the Colombian national squad in that South American country.

The pressure on Robinho rose in 2004. That's when some of his teammates moved on to play soccer in Europe. He was up to the task. He led Santos with 32 goals and its second Brazilian title in three years. He was on top of the soccer world. But a scary incident that year made Robinho forget all about soccer.

It was November 6, 2004. His mother Marina was cooking for friends in the Brazilian coastal town of Praia Grande. Suddenly, gunmen burst into the house. They stuffed Marina into a car. They locked her hosts in a bathroom and sped off. She had been kidnapped! Robinho was allowed to leave his team and fly home to the rest of his family.

The kidnappers were hoping to take advantage of Robinho's wealth. He was earning $500,000 a year from Santos and through sponsors. That was far less than many European stars earned. But it was enough to allow

While Robinho sat out and waited for the release of his mother, fans and supporters gathered at Santos' games to show support. The sign reads "Robinho, we are praying for you."

FORÇA ROBINHO.
ESTAMOS REZANDO
POR VOCÊ!
EDSON CESAR ALUMA - Z L

him to move family members to a fine section of Santos. Robinho was red-eyed when he spoke to reporters after the kidnapping.

"I hope this ends well, with my mum returning and me playing football," he said. "I ask for understanding and to be left in peace."

Marina was one of five mothers of Brazilian players kidnapped in five months. The kidnappers demanded ransom money from Robinho. They ordered him to stop playing soccer. They sent him a video showing that they had shaved her head. They threatened to harm her. Robinho sent them the money. Marina was released after forty-one days in captivity.

The ordeal did not affect Robinho's play when he returned to the soccer field. He performed well for Brazil in the 2005 FIFA Confederations Cup. He scored a goal in a first-round win over Greece. He added another in a tie against Japan. Soon he was celebrating a championship with his teammates. Brazil easily defeated South American rival Argentina in the finals.

Santos wanted to keep Robinho. But the twenty-one-year-old superstar knew it would be safer in Europe. He also knew he could earn much more money. And that's just what he did. Robinho signed a $30 million contract with Spanish soccer power Real Madrid CF in July 2005. Real Madrid had won a bidding war against several other clubs. Soon Robinho was moving himself and his family to the Spanish capital city of Madrid.

He arrived a month later to great fanfare. He gave an exhibition to his new fans. He thrilled a crowd of eight thousand in Madrid with an amazing display of his ballhandling skills. He balanced one ball after another on his back. He flicked them over his shoulder and kicked them into the stands. Fans raced out onto the field to embrace him.

'Today we are going to present one of the great players in the world," said Real Madrid president Florentino Pérez. "[Soccer] can be many things but one of the most important is the spectacle it provides, and it is in this aspect of fantasy football that Robinho excels. It hasn't been an easy road for him to come to Real Madrid, but I think he's chosen the perfect team and the perfect league for him to demonstrate his skills. Robinho's Real Madrid dream begins here."

The young man called the "Stepover King" promised to use the moves he made famous for his new team.

"I hope to use a few of my trademark (step-overs) against my opponents while I'm here," he told the fans with a smile. "But above all I want to help make Real Madrid a champion team and win a lot of trophies."

Robinho was about to make good on his promise.

Robinho took control in the title game against Corinthians in 2002. He did everything he could to defend opposing player Rogério.

More Goals, More Championships

Robinho faced a new world upon arriving in Madrid in 2005. He had moved to a new country thousands of miles from home. He had grown up speaking Portuguese, but the people of Madrid spoke Spanish. He was about to compete against much better players and teams on the soccer fields of Europe.

He also had to manage immense wealth for the first time in his life. Many athletes that grow up poor spend their time and money unwisely when they become rich. Some fall into bad habits such as taking drugs or alcohol.

Robinho was only far from his native Brazil in miles. Bringing his family with him to Madrid made him feel

Robinho shown being introduced as the newest star to join powerhouse Real Madrid.

close to home. He wanted to prove that he could compete at the highest level of his sport. There was great pressure. The media was still calling him the next Pelé. He found it hard to live up to that comparison. He spoke about that after signing with Real Madrid.

"They compare me a lot with Pelé," he said. "He played in Santos. … But Pelé is unmatched. I know it's very hard to reach the level I did, but I hope to be successful."

He was successful winning the hearts of soccer fans. He organized a charity match in December 2006. He returned to Santos with other Brazilian players now competing in Europe. He asked fans to bring food to be donated to hungry people in his country. The gesture showed that he had a special place in his heart for Santos. It would remain there forever.

"It is a great joy to return to the Santo stadium, my second home, and to help Brazil's charities at the same time," he said.

Robinho began his Real Madrid career with a bang. He scored three goals in his first four matches for his new team. But he added just three goals in his next 27 matches. He finished his first season with just 11 goals and 5 assists in 51 matches.   He was not as successful as he hoped. He did play a big role in the success of a winning team. But he did not perform to the level many expected. They assumed he would have dominated. Robinho was named "Man of the Match" in a win over Spanish rival FC Barcelona early the next year. He tallied two goals and two assists in his first two matches to help Brazil qualify for the World Cup. He managed just one assist and no goals in World Cup play that summer. He was left on the bench for one entire contest.

When he returned to Real Madrid, manager Fabio Capello did not even place him on the starting team. During one 23-match stretch in early 2007, he scored just one goal. His career was going in the wrong direction.

Robinho was too talented to stay down for long. He suddenly caught fire. He scored three of his team's five goals in three straight league victories. He finished the year with 5 goals in his last 12 games to help Real Madrid win the league championship.

Robinho flies over his opponent to save the ball from going out of bounds. Robinho has the ability to be a real game changer when he is at his best.

He maintained his momentum the following season. He recorded seven goals and six assists in one sizzling stretch in the fall of 2007. His team won every match in which he scored during that hot streak. Robinho went on another tear in the winter with eight goals and four assists in one fifteen-game period. His scoring explosion helped Real Madrid capture its second straight league title.

There was just one problem. Robinho had become unhappy with his team. His three-year contract was nearing an end. He was upset that Real Madrid would not allow him to play for Brazil in the 2006 Summer Olympics.

He also did not believe Real Madrid was working hard enough to keep him. He felt snubbed when the team declared its interest in signing Manchester United

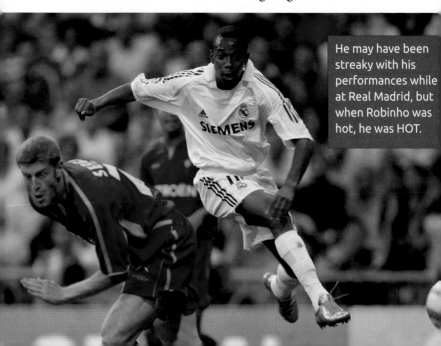

He may have been streaky with his performances while at Real Madrid, but when Robinho was hot, he was HOT.

superstar Cristiano Ronaldo. Robinho would not play another match for Real Madrid.

"I had some good moments in Madrid," Robinho said years later. "The only bad thing about my three-year stay at the club was the way I left it. The club was trying to sign [Ronaldo], and they didn't appear to care about me."

Real Madrid's former president Ramón Calderón promised to begin talks with Robinho about a new contract during the 2007–08 season. But they never took place.

"When they realized the deal wasn't going to be made on that summer of 2008, [they] tried to fix things with me, but I wasn't interested in staying anymore," Robinho said. "I felt neglected throughout the entire process."

Robinho was still a highly sought after commodity. His standout performance in the 2007 Copa América was still fresh in the minds of club owners. Other top division European football clubs were hoping to sign the Brazilian superstar. Two of them—Manchester City FC and Chelsea FC—were based in England.

Robinho had asked for a transfer to Chelsea in the summer of 2008. He signed instead with Manchester City. He believed that team could develop into a champion. He was also excited to join Brazilian friends Jô and Elano, who were playing for Manchester City.

Calderón explained why he and Real Madrid coach Bernd Schuster allowed Robinho to leave for England. Calderón believed that bad advice from others was making the young star unhappy.

"It's a decision agreed by all the coaching staff, who understand it is best for the player and for the club," he said. "Schuster thought until yesterday that he could recover the player, but that has not been the case. Every time I have spoken with [Robinho] he was very sad, crying and asking to leave Spain. Real Madrid are more important than any one player. He's a great kid, but badly advised."

Robinho was about to start a new chapter in his life. It was not going to be a happy one. He would soon yearn for a return to his beloved Brazil.

One of Robinho's mentors during his time with Real Madrid was teammate David Beckham.

Hot and Cold Robinho

It was a late October afternoon in 2008. More than forty-four thousand fans braved the cold, rainy weather to watch their favorite team play at City of Manchester Stadium.

Robinho put on a show they would never forget. He had started his stint with Manchester City red-hot. He had tallied six goals and three assists in the eleven games. But he was on fire against Stoke City on that chilly day.

He secured a pass off the head of teammate Ched Evans and booted it into the net for his first goal. He separated from a defender and blasted the ball past the goaltender for a second goal. Soon the goaltender was diving in vain as

While playing for Manchester City, Robinho made the most of his time on the pitch, proving that he deserved to be a starter.

Robinho kicked the ball past him again. Robinho sprinted down the field in celebration. He had scored all three goals in a 3–0 victory.

Manchester City manager Mark Hughes was glowing in his praise of his new star.

"[Robinho] was excellent today," he said. "It wasn't just his goals that impressed me, it was his [soccer] intelligence. He always knew where his teammates were and knew how to hurt the opposition. Great players know what angles to attack from and what to do to have maximum impact. His awareness of players around him showed his quality.

"He is key to what we are doing here and maybe he hasn't felt that before. He has responded in the right way, the crowd adores him and everybody here loves him."

Robinho gave them a reason to keep loving him for the next two months. He scored six more goals in the next eleven games. He recorded two goals and an assist in a 5–1 win over Hull City. But when 2009 rolled around, he became as cold as the winter weather. Robinho did not score a goal in the next nineteen games. He did tally a goal in three straight matches at the end of the season.

Manchester City finished the year with a poor 15–18 record in Premier League play. Some blamed Robinho. Others felt the team would have been much worse without him. After all, his 14 goals ranked fourth in the league.

The next year started well—he scored six goals for Brazil in World Cup qualifying and in the Confederations Cup. But his return to Manchester City was a disaster. He

Even though he was not happy playing for Manchester City, Robinho still went out and played like a champion every match.

When Manchester City let Robinho go back to Santos on a loan, he started to have fun again, and started playing like a superstar again!

was out for weeks with an ankle injury. He did not earn the respect of new manager Roberto Mancini. He sat on the bench for entire matches. He did not start any games. He scored just one goal.

His personal life was faring better. Robinho married childhood sweetheart Vivian Guglielmetti in July 2009. The couple had been dating for twelve years and had a nineteen-month-old son named Robson, Jr. Their best man in the wedding was Marcelo Teixeira. That is who signed him to his first contract with Santos, which is where Robinho wanted to return. He was unhappy in England.

Manchester City granted his request. He showed his joy with great performances on the field. His return to Brazil in February 2010 was marked by an amazing scoring display. He scored five goals in his first six matches—all of which Santos won. The team also won five of the next six matches in which Robinho scored. He played so well that he was named to the 2010 Brazil World Cup team.

Robinho did not let his country down. He tallied two goals and an assist in four games. He scored his team's only goal in a 2–1 loss to the Netherlands that knocked Brazil out of the event. But he could not stay in his home country. He was only on loan from Manchester City. The club could not make a deal to keep him with Santos.

He did not want to return to England. He had decided that he yearned to play in Italy. He was given his wish on September 1, 2010. That was the day he signed with

AC Milan. He was thrilled to join fellow Brazilian stars Ronaldinho and Alexandre Pato on that club.

"I know that the Brazilian players on the team will give me a great hand in adapting to the team," Robinho said. "I will work very hard to make the fans very happy. I want to bring so much joy to them."

Robinho was true to his word. He played in 45 matches—more than any teammate. His 15 goals placed third on the team. And he helped AC Milan win the Italian Serie A title. He tied for the team lead with 14 goals in league play.

It appeared that Robinho was destined for greatness in Italy. But bad luck would get in the way.

Not OK for AC Milan

Robinho wanted to take his momentum and run with it. Second son Gianluca had been born in April 2011. He had enjoyed a great first season for AC Milan. He was ready in the summer of 2011 to perform even better.

But Robinho could not perform at all for two months. A thigh injury kept him out of action from August to October. He wasted no time booting the ball into the net upon his return though. He scored a goal in his first game back to help his team beat U.S. Città di Palermo in their first league game of the season.

Robinho played hot and cold all year. He tallied two goals and three assists during one nine-game stretch in late

Whenever he can, Robinho finds time to teach his sons a thing or two about soccer. Here he is showing Robson, Jr., some moves during a practice with the Brazilian national team.

2011. He added three goals and four assists in a four-game tear in early 2012. Yet, he also went long periods without scoring.

He finished that season third on the team with 11 goals and first with 10 assists. But he had not recorded a goal or assist for Brazil in the 2011 America Cup. That was a surprise. After all, he had dominated that event four years earlier. Robinho also did not play well enough to earn a spot on Brazil's 2012 Summer Olympic team.

Robinho did continue to lend his time and energy to charity work. He thrilled the crowd with his ball skills in the "Christmas Without Hunger 2011" match. He showed off the dribbling wizardry that had made him famous.

He needed to get off to a good start for AC Milan the next season. What happened instead was strange, sad, and bad luck. He hurt his thigh in August 2012, a year after he injured it the first time. He was hurt during the first league game and did not play for a month.

Robinho bounced back well from his thigh injury in 2011, but not this time. He did not tally a goal or assist in the first five games upon his return. He was often not used as a starter. He hurt his thigh again in October and missed another month.

The season featured few bright spots. Robinho earned a rare start in December. He responded with a goal and assist in a 4–2 win over Torino FC. In that game, he flashed the talent that had once made him a star. He faked out a defender and blasted the ball past the diving goaltender. The ball settled into the right corner of the net.

Robinho was scoreless in seven games and did not even play in five others. Some people in the media criticized him. They even wondered how hard he was trying on the field. One writer questioned him in 2013 after Robinho played poorly in a loss to rival Barcelona.

"It's fair to say Robinho hasn't delivered on the grandest stage," he wrote. "He should have done, he has the ability, he just doesn't seem to care."

Rumors swirled that Robinho wanted to leave Milan. AC Milan head Adriano Galliani tried to end those rumors. He said in January 2013 that Robinho hoped to stay. The only place he would accept a transfer would be to his beloved Santos. Galliani tried to work out a deal with that club, but it fell through.

The rumors did not end there. One Santos official said he planned to talk to Robinho in the summer of 2013 about a return to the team.

Robinho had settled down in Milan. He had yearned to leave Real Madrid and Manchester City. But despite his struggles in 2012 and 2013, he expressed a desire to stay in Italy. He even spoke about wanting to sign a new deal with AC Milan.

"A new contract?" he asked. "We can certainly talk about that. First of all, I want to end the season in the best way and then we can talk about these things. ... I never asked to leave the club. It was Santos who came in for me.

Robinho blasts a goal right past the diving Catania goalkeeper.

Robinho hopes to play in Milan for many more years, and with his most recent contract extension, he will be there until at least 2016.

I spoke to my family about it and we have decided to stay. … There's nothing I'm lacking here at Milan."

Robinho believed the only thing he was lacking was good health. He wanted to play a big role for AC Milan in its quest to win another title. He was twenty-nine years old. He felt he could still help a team to a championship and that all he needed was a chance. And a chance is what he was given. In July 2013, Robinho was given a contract extension with AC Milan that would keep him there until June 2016.

Age and injuries had taken away some of the skills that once had him being compared to the great Pelé. But pride would not allow Robinho to give up. And even if he never returned to the form that made him great, there would be wonderful memories. Millions of soccer fans would always remember the amazing moves that made him special.

Career Highlights and Awards

- Campeonato Brasileiro Série A champion (with Santos): 2002, 2004

- CONCACAF Gold Cup: Silver (Runners-up) 2003

- Copa Libertadores de América: Silver (Runners-up) 2003

- World Soccer Young Player of the Year Award: 2004–05

- Bola de Ouro Award: 2005

- FIFA Confederations Cup champion: 2005, 2009

- La Liga champion (with Real Madrid): 2006–07, 2007–08

- Copa América champion: 2007

- Copa América Golden Ball (Best Player of the Tournament): 2007

- Copa América Golden Shoe (Top scorer): 2007

- Supercopa de España champion (with Real Madrid): 2008

- Campeonato Paulista champion (with Santos): 2010

- Copa do Brasil champion (with Santos): 2010

- Serie A champion (with AC Milan): 2010–11

- Supercoppa Italiana champion (with AC Milan): 2011

- Signed his professional contract with Santos FC in 2002 at the age of eighteen.

INTERNET ADDRESSES

Robinho's Official Site

<http://www.robinhooficial.com.br/en/>

AC Milan Homepage

<http://www.acmilan.com/en>

FIFA Official Site

<http://www.fifa.com/>

INDEX